#47ThingsILearned

For Mom.

Thank you for
        making me,
        teaching me harmony,
        loving me,
        and the sammich.

INTRODUCTION

WHAT I LEARNED WRITING #47ThingsILearned

I learned quite a lot when I wrote this book. I learned that writing a book is an excellent way to learn how to write a book. I learned that some of the material in my personal cache is commonplace, a comfortable way to start a conversation. I learned that some of the esoteric stuff floating around in my noggin is kerfluffling and also serves, miraculously enough, as a way to start a conversation. And I reminded myself that learning is born of doing, of discovery.

We learn by enlisting our senses. We learn visually, aurally, viscerally, by rolling up our sleeves and digging in. We learn kinetically, taking stumbling halting steps or running full-tilt-boogie.

We learn by making mistakes. We learn the hard way. We learn by encouraging our brain to get confused enough to be frustrated enough to fail often enough to find success.

We learn by synthesizing and personalizing, putting information and experience into our own words and ways of being. We learn by being curious, interested, and involved. We learn with the help of our friends. We cement our learning by taking action, by reaching out and teaching others.

#47ThingsILearned is designed as a book of action, tangible packets of inspiration and accessible creative solutions. A book to do.

Peppered throughout you'll find Consideration Challenges, activities to help you connect, to engage your heart and mind, and urge you to discover.

So grab a pen or a pencil or your favorite crayon – I'm partial to atomic tangerine – and prepare to write in this book. Make it your own. Add your brilliant insight and personal musings. Draw, scribble, underline, doodle, highlight, take note, and take charge of your own learning.

We've got a lot of discovery to do.

#1

Feeling broken?
Smile.
It fixes your face.

Broken is a bummer, until we remember that feelings are convertible and we hold the power.

In purely non-medical terms, an honest smile sends happy synapses coursing through the system, rewiring sensations.

Close your eyes. Breathe out slowly. Think of something that brings you joy. Breathe in the idea and smile.

Happy fix!

CONSIDERATION CHALLENGE
Meditate on this simple truth.
You don't have to be perfect, but you do have to get to the next step. Sometimes that next step is fueled by the burst of energy only a smile can provide. So give yourself a break and then get back in the game.
Thirty seconds. Go.

#2

**Shakespeare was correct.
Sleep
really does knit
the raveled sleeve of care.**

If I am overwhelmed with feelings, ill-equipped, out of sorts, slogging through a seemingly unsolvable problem, or half-a-click away from clicking "send" on an e-mail I'll likely want to recall in the morning, I go to bed and sleep on it.

A solid night's rest is an excellent cure, and everything looks better in fresh light.

CONSIDERATION CHALLENGE
Are you running right up to bedtime perplexed, troubled, and spinning without a solution? Your subconscious is a stellar problem solver, excited to wake you up in the morning with fresh clarity. Rewire your brain by setting aside the burdens of the day 30 minutes before tucking in. Shift focus. Instead of the high-tech, illuminated, battery-operated flat thing, wind down with a book.
What book will it be?

#3

If you want
to go to a party,
you may need to ask
for an invitation.

Have you stood on the periphery, watching other folks immersed in what looked like full-on fun? Figure they have the inside edge, a special sheen of popularity, or a backstage pass?

What they actually have is gumption enough to decide to be involved and the guts to dismiss their self-consciousness. If you want to be part of the party, project, solution, or adventure, invite yourself, showing up at the door with a smile and a suggestion:
"I'm here! Let's get this party started!"

If there isn't a party, throw one.
Invite everyone.

Consideration Challenge
Look around. You may notice you are not the only one standing on the fringe, feeling shy. Hold out a hand. Who will you invite?

#4

Let others
be your mirror.

There is beauty in being blindsided by an unexpected compliment that awakens our assessment of "mighty and awesome."

Staring at ourselves full on, fussing over every carbuncle or straining to glimpse… that… one… spot we can never quite see isn't nearly as enchanting or educational as the perspective of people who genuinely care for us and will tell the truth.

CONSIDERATION CHALLENGE
Are you skilled at accepting
an unexpected compliment?
Practice listening wholeheartedly and
responding gratefully to caring words.

#5

Tend a garden.

One of the best summers of my life was spent in the yard, doing my best to live like my G'ma Elvene.

She was happy.
She grew flowers and cooked jam.
She laughed a lot and worried little.
She made the most out of what she had.
She was nice.
Her garden was bursting with the happy faces of yellow blossoms and hospitality.

CONSIDERATION CHALLENGE
Hey Sunshine! Ask yourself…
What are you cultivating now for others to harvest in the future?

#6

Everyone is sentimental about something.

A chipped pottery cup. An earring whose mate has long been lost. A best friend who also happens to be a cat. The world's most mangy pair of socks. A song sung off-key.

When we give a heartfelt nod to what tugs at our own heartstrings, we are more inclined to respect the genuine affections of others.

CONSIDERATION CHALLENGE
True Confessions!
What tugs at your heartstrings?

#7

Good manners
go a long way.

On any quest, the gracious guest finds open
the most interesting doors.

Respectful etiquette is always welcome.
And it never hurts to bring a hostess gift.

CONSIDERATION CHALLENGE
What are three of your favorite mannerly
gestures or actions?

#8

**It is easier to
tell the truth
than remember a lie.**

It may seem tough to choke out the truth early on, but a lie becomes increasingly tangled over time, is hard to swallow, knots the belly, and upsets everyone's digestion.

CONSIDERATION CHALLENGE

Find someone who will tell you the truth and dare you to be better.
Who is it?
Ask him or her to be your mentor.

#9

**Nothing turns
a pretty girl ugly
faster than mean.**

Gorgeous turns gorgon at the heavy hand of bullying behavior. Mean is fast and sharp, shaping in unflattering ways.

Witness likewise, the way kindness caresses our feature and how a hand outstretched in generosity is graceful. Listen to the sweet sound of a loving word.

True of everyone, fellas too... courtesy is where beauty blooms.

CONSIDERATION CHALLENGE
If you find yourself speaking unkindly about yourself or others, fire your inner critic and cultivate the ability to articulate the positive.
Say three encouraging things.
Yes, out loud.

#10

**You go where you look.
So look where you go.**

Consider a sacrosanct tenet of the motorcycling set: The motorcycle will follow your line of sight. If you look ahead at the endless ribbon of horizon, to the potential of the open road and the possibility of the future, that is where you will go. If you get distracted and look over there, at the cows…

(Wow! Look! Cows!)

…well… that ends up no fun for either you, or the cows.

Consideration Challenge
Much like a fortune cookie, you are packed full of unexpected wisdom.
Write the fortune for your future.

#11

**You can't fill
an emotional hole
with a physical object.**

Heartbroken? Hug your beloveds.
Hug them and love them and tell them they
are wonderful and perfect for you. Look at
them and breathe them in and listen. Then
hug them again.

A shiny new sports car or pair of sky-high
stilettos may be delightful distractions, but
they fall short in matters of the heart and soul.

Consideration Challenge
Set a date to spend live-and-in-person time
with a person you admire and esteem.
Who is it? When?

#12

**If you want
to be interesting,
be interested.**

Every person, place, and thing has a story to tell. If you are caring and attentive, eventually the story will be told to you.

Taking an honest and ardent interest in the people, places, and things around you is everyday archaeology.

You'll have adventures.
You'll become increasingly interesting.
People will want to hear your story.

Consideration Challenge

At your next social gathering, practice being an enthusiastic listener.
What did you discover and how might others' experiences inspire your next adventure?

#13

I have never regretted
biting my tongue
and biding my time.

Ever experience that moment when you fling the perfect scathing phrase to win the fight?

Yeah. Me neither.

Sometimes it takes years to confabulate a counterattack more linguistically compelling than "Oh yeah?"

I've found it more graceful to skip the cutting commentary, let the dust settle, seek understanding, and give reasonable dignity the opportunity to prevail.

CONSIDERATION CHALLENGE
Would your perspective change if you had more information?
Learn about something you find frustrating.

#14

Always wear sunscreen.
And your seatbelt.

Two of the four basic promises my mom asked of me when, at 17, I left home for the wide wide world.

Smart.
Easy.

When someone who loves you asks you to take care of yourself, do it.

CONSIDERATION CHALLENGE
What is the best advice you have received?
What is your favorite advice to share?

#15

It's hard to be angry while you're dancing like Snoopy from Peanuts.

Try it.

The next time you are steaming mad, stop.
Plant your feet firmly on the floor.
Take a deep breath and bust out a Snoopy
groove. You don't actually need dance skills,
just a sense of "shake it" abandon. Extra
credit for moving your feet and singing along.

It's always good to have a sure-fire way to
pattern-interrupt a bad mood.

CONSIDERATION CHALLENGE
Make a good-old-fashioned mix-tape.
What songs are on your "shake it" playlist?

#16

Birthday cake tastes better without a fork.

Celebrate with abandon.
A self-imposed cake face-plant provides
full culinary effect of your favorite frosting.
And you will laugh.

(Mind the candles!)

CONSIDERATION CHALLENGE
Don't wait for a specific date.
Host an unbirthday celebration, complete with
silly hats, noisemakers, and cake!

#17

**If you ask,
"What do YOU think I
should do?"
people will tell you.**

On the days when I am in need of
slap-myself-on-the-forehead
why-didn't-I-think-of-that brilliance,
I take a risk and enlist the next chance person
I encounter, specifically and simply asking:
"What do YOU think I should do?"

Whether standing across the checkout
counter at the grocery store or in line at the
coffee shop, we find friendly faces in
unexpected places. When queried, people
will often blurt out the idea or task by which
they themselves are made most excited,
which is a great jumping off point for taking
action in our own lives.

Daring inspiration is everywhere.

Consideration Challenge
Ask three people,
"What do YOU think I should do?"
What did they say?

#18

You catch more flies with honey than vinegar.

Short and sweet simple social science:
Kindness is magnetic.
Cruelty is repulsive.

CONSIDERATION CHALLENGE
List seven kinds of kindness.

#19

You are
stronger than you think.

Much like the Incredible Hulk, you can do amazing things when your adrenaline gets going. The key is learning how to unleash strength with intention and harness it to a beneficial result.

CONSIDERATION CHALLENGE

What are your automatic, irrepressible "default" strengths?
Gimme five.

#20

If you're happy and you know it shout it out.

True confessions.

I intentionally yammer out my everyday thank you list while I'm in the shower waiting for the hair-conditioner to work. Some days I'm super happy and croon the list as a silly song. Some days I'm grouchy as all get-out and can barely grind out gratitude for hot water, which reminds me I'm fortunate to have water at all. Awareness sets in, and the list gets longer. I do my best to remember to do this every day.

Invariably, the days I remember to do this become better days.

CONSIDERATION CHALLENGE
Set a timer and invest three minutes articulating reasons why you are grateful.
Yes. Out loud

#21

**Bring your best
and enough to share.**

Plenty.
And always room for another at the table.

In my journeys I've been blessed to share in the boundless banquet on a beggar's budget in China, the beach bonfire in St. Lucia that fed everyone, the ambrosia of Alabama banana pudding served in an ad-hoc restaurant in the front room of a trailer home on a dead-end dirt road and found that "enough" appears when we move closer.

Hospitality.
Set an extra place.
Share.

CONSIDERATION CHALLENGE
Hey cupcake!
What are you bringing?
Fill in the blank.
My "best" is...

#22

**Candle wax
will loosen a sticky zipper.**
(I kid you not.)

There's a reason advice columnists enjoy our enduring affection and we look for direction from folks who've been around the block. New-fangled is nice, but sometimes the old-fashioned remedies are best.

If you are stuck, ask for help. Someone you know may have already experienced the same problem, and worked out a solution.

(P.S. A little bit of beeswax or the end of an unlit candle rubbed gently along the teeth of a zipper will smooth the works.)

CONSIDERATION CHALLENGE

What is your favorite old-fashioned remedy? Poll three people from different generations, backgrounds, or cultures about theirs.

#23

PIE.

Pie is for sharing, and for storytelling.

G'ma Elvene served pie for breakfast at her table, making one, two, three on an afternoon, setting them to cool on the front porch ledge as an invitation to tomorrow's meal.

One day, the neighbor's pointy-nosed dog stopped by and snooted a perfect circle out of the center of each one, leaving room for a legendary story.

Cook up reason to gather and gab, linger and laugh.

CONSIDERATION CHALLENGE
Ask someone about his or her legendary story.

#24

**If you don't know, ask.
Take good notes.**

The test of time proves true:
The best information bears repeating.

On the first day of class, our junior-high
history teacher opened by saying his lectures
were a lot like life, and that the most important
lessons show up more than once. Then he
told us how to ace his class: be inquisitive,
attentive, and take note of recurring themes,
because they were guaranteed to be on the
test. His painstaking explanations helped us
learn, ensured we developed listening as a
vital skill, and effectively gave us the answer
well in advance of the question.

Someone you know knows the answer to your
question, and they are willing to tell you.

Be smart. Write it down.
Teach someone else.

CONSIDERATION CHALLENGE
Get ready now for the next lesson.
Have a notebook handy.

#25

Sit in the nice chair.

I own a "nice chair" in which I seldom sat, fearing it too precious to use. One day a dear friend dropped by, plopped down, scooted around, tucked in, put up her feet, and grinned.

I found myself made quite happy by her enjoyment of the "nice chair" and her ability to use with intense satisfaction the nice thing now, rather than saving it for an unforeseeable future.

Encouraged, I began a practice of sitting in the "nice chair" and found the view better, primarily because I can see I am not wasting my resources by hoarding them.

CONSIDERATION CHALLENGE
What have you been saving "for good?"
Use it.
If you no longer have a need for it, donate it.

#26

YYURYYUBICURYY4Me.

G'ma Alice inscribed this line in a cryptic card I received as a kid, my first time away at sleep-away camp. My cabin mates and I spent so much time teaming up to decipher it, enlisting other kids and making friends over the mystery, we forgot entirely about our differences or being homesick.

Sometimes our first reaction to something we don't understand is "I don't like that."
I've learned to suspend judgment and say instead, "I'm still learning."

(Feeling confused? That's your brain, getting curious.
If you need help figuring the answer, turn to the end of the book,
just beyond #47.)

CONSIDERATION CHALLENGE
Tease your brain.
Set aside pre-conceived notions and
research something
enigmatic or puzzling.
What will it be?

#27

A book is a passport.

Curiosity and a library card can take you anywhere. The bookstore beckons. Breathe in the smell of glue and paper and cardboard and coffee as you walk in. Feast on the bright gleam of a new page. Sway to the music of words playing out in your imagination.

Literature brings the rush of undiscovered adventures as you embark on the first paragraph.

Read.

CONSIDERATION CHALLENGE
What book changed your life?
Keep an extra copy handy to share.

#28

We learn most efficiently
when we are either
utterly terrified
or joyously laughing.
I choose laughing.

Intellect thrives on adventure and the unexpected. Laughter encourages elasticity. The brain gets excited to adapt in extreme circumstances, seeking to absorb as much information as possible.

When you laugh, you learn.

CONSIDERATION CHALLENGE
Humor and optimism go hand in hand.
Reignite your funny bone and your brain.
Think back to the adventures that made you giggle as a kid.
What were they and how could you put levity back into play today?

#29

**A lot of stuff
is none of my business.**

First, let's focus on what is our business; investing energy to positively impact that which we value most.

Gossip? Worry? Distraction? Meh. Boring. Let's get back to business.

CONSIDERATION CHALLENGE
What daily distraction is keeping you from making distance in mission-critical areas? Give it a time-out for today.

#30

**Leave it better
than we found it.**

We can put our fingerprint on the future.
Positively.

Pick up trash along the hiking trail. Close the gate carelessly left open. Open the door for someone whose hands are full. Lend a hand to the task at hand.

Contribute.

CONSIDERATION CHALLENGE
How do you leave tomorrow better than you found today?
What is your legacy?

#31

Something to do.
Something to love.
Something to hope for.

The idea of "do good and feel better" is attributed to many, with good reason.

Employ the hands.
Employ the heart.
Employ the brain.

Doing is more than a delightful diversion; it is positive propulsion.

CONSIDERATION CHALLENGE
Pay it forward.
Ease someone else's path.

#32

Never negotiate against yourself.

Understand the discerning line between yes and no. Realize what serves you well and how to respect your best interests. Find your voice and know when to hold your tongue. Stand up for yourself and stand firm.

CONSIDERATION CHALLENGE
When was the last time you catalogued your awesomeness?
Take the time to respect your talents.
Update your resume.

#33

**Making
the same bad choice
multiple times
does not make it
a better choice.**

I'm stubborn.

Sometimes my ego and I struggle together, stumbling down poorly-lit old pathways that lead nowhere, or pitching a fit trying to fix something beyond repair.

Best to back up, own up, reset, point all that pith in a positive direction, and take a new tack.

CONSIDERATION CHALLENGE
What choice is no longer serving you?
What positive action will you use to replace it?

#34

Handwritten thank you notes are always in style.

Scribbled on fancy monogrammed stationery or painstakingly inscribed on the inside of a flattened, empty, turned inside-out to-go cup… your words, in your hand, given to another in gratitude are a token worth cherishing.

CONSIDERATION CHALLENGE
Handwrite a thank you note.
Hand-deliver or stamp and send it.

#35

"Famous and
quite wonderful"
is a state of mind that
inspires a way of being.

Inspiration is contagious.

If you believe you are famous and quite wonderful, you will behave in famous and quite wonderful ways.

Start an epidemic of awesome.
Use your powers for good.

CONSIDERATION CHALLENGE
KAPOW!
What is your superpower?
Who benefits?

#36

**It's cool
to introduce cool people
to other cool people.**

Good faith. Word of mouth.
Recommendation. Seal of approval.

An address book is less about digits than
knowing what folks do. Connect someone
who is a master in his or her craft to someone
in need.

CONSIDERATION CHALLENGE
Share the wealth.
Update your contact list to include detail.
Dial in on people's talents.
Make introductions.

#37

The secrets to success should not be kept secret.

A shared storehouse of great ideas and vital discoveries makes everyone better.

Bring your gift. Give it freely.

CONSIDERATION CHALLENGE
If you stacked up your hard-won learnings, what would be the top three?

#38

**Step away
from the computer.**

Back in the day, we used to gaze at the world through a wonderful low-tech flat thing called a window. In clement weather the window could be opened, allowing us to hear, smell, feel, and even taste the world. If we were daring and imaginative, we could escape into the outside, crawling through the window and shimmying down a tree, or lowering ourselves to safety via a rope fashioned from our bed sheets. Or, we could simply walk out the front door.

The computer is 12 inches away.
The world is closer.
Bust beyond virtual and into the real world.

CONSIDERATION CHALLENGE
While you are backing up your data, reboot your brain. Put down the high-tech, illuminated, battery-operated flat thing.
Go outside.

#39

We keep going
because we keep going.

Sometimes the shocking shifts of life toss us into a state of stasis. When we are stuck, motionless or immobilized, the tiniest twitch of encouragement can reignite energy.

I find that the people who enjoy the most vibrant longevity are those who dig in and devote themselves to sharing the beauty of their individual contribution. They perpetuate momentum by shaking off life's setbacks, embracing tough lessons, and getting back in the groove.

Find it. Move it. Shake it. Groove it.

New is now. Movement builds momentum. Momentum generates sustainable success.

CONSIDERATION CHALLENGE
What obstacle have you overcome?
How will you use what you have learned to spark enthusiasm in another?

#40

Stretch.

An inquisitive mind is excellent inoculation against ennui. Fresh perspective is the perfect prescription for inspiration.

Ply every fiber to the fullest extent.
Mix unexpected elements.
Try new things.
Be curious.

CONSIDERATION CHALLENGE

Excite your brain with an inspiration break and find a new thought-leader to follow. Who did you choose and why?

#41

A good scrub in the tub makes it all better.

When I am woebegone, kerfluffled, baffled, or bamboozled by my day, I give myself a time-out in the tub. Steam and soap and a song or two can reset a compass star and right a listing ship.

(Extra-credit for a rubber ducky.)

CONSIDERATION CHALLENGE
Give yourself a time-out and a treat.
What will it be?

#42

**A sandwich
is more delicious
when someone you love
makes it for you.**

My favorite kind of meal is a simple one made with care, because it offers the opportunity to appreciate the result of affectionate work.

Have you lately been the object of fond attention?

Return the favor.

(Tuna on sourdough, with a dill pickle and potato chips, is especially nice.)

CONSIDERATION CHALLENGE
Return a good turn.
Who will be the recipient of your favor and how will you deliver it?

#43

The cure for "sad"
is showing kindness
to another.

Feeling is not the same as being.

As a self-described "heart on her sleeve" kind of gal, I'm made happy by the understanding that feelings are temporary and replaceable sensations. If I am drowning in a feeling I don't fancy, I throw myself a lifeline by taking action and being of service. Being is an opportunity to change my condition and the quality of my experience. When I banish a sensation of "sad" by focusing on others, I feel better.

CONSIDERATION CHALLENGE

Are you beset by not-so-nice feelings?
Set them aside and fill that space with the satisfying sensation that comes from being of service.
Go be a force of good in the life of another.
Who will benefit, and how?

#44

**You can sing
(many, if not all)
Emily Dickinson poems
to the tune
"Yellow Rose of Texas."**

"Mashups" are nothing new.

Music and literature have crossed dividing lines for ages, connecting us culturally in unexpected and artistic ways.

I expect now you will learn a new song, a new poem, or both.

CONSIDERATION CHALLENGE
Try it.
Sing an Emily Dickinson poem to the tune of "Yellow Rose of Texas" and laugh.
Then go make your own mashup.

#45

**Tiny victories
stack up
to make a mountain.**

Every victory, no matter how small, helps us stand taller.

My true confession is that waiting to be "perfect" was an excuse I made to leave things half-finished, until I reminded myself that every win is worthwhile.

Is today the day you'll finish your big project? Maybe your stellar conquest is as complex as getting out the door with all your stuff and socks that match, or as simple as taking a shower. Perhaps you'll high-five yourself for running a 5k, or crossing the laundry pile finish line. Will you tackle a daunting overdue task, or be brave enough to try a different kind of salsa on your burrito?

From commonplace to colossal success, know there is value in every victory.

CONSIDERATION CHALLENGE
Celebrate a victory from today.
Plan one for tomorrow.

#46

Ninjas!

There was a time in my life when I dug myself a pretty deep hole of forlorn and alone. When it was time to haul myself out, I called on the people in my life I call Ninjas to lend a hand.

I reach out to my Ninjas for a high five and a victory dance, a shoulder to cry on, a slap upside the head, or, in the middle of the night, to say "bring a shovel, come quick."

CONSIDERATION CHALLENGE
List your Ninjas.
Call them all. Reconnect the dots and resurrect relationships.
Fill them in and hear them out, offer and ask, simply say hello, I need you.

#47

You are loved.

You.
You are.
You are loved.

CONSIDERATION CHALLENGE
Who?
Who do?
Who do you love?
Go. Let 'em know.

What is YYURYYUBICURYY4ME?

Too wise you are.
Too wise you be.
I see you are, too wise for me.

It's a Brain Teaser!
The purpose of riddles is to make your thinker
curious, interested, involved, considerate,
interactive, challenged, and inspired.

Conclusion

Upon the auspicious morning of my 47th birthday it dawned on me that in some circles 47 is considered the "quintessential number."

quin·tes·sen·tial
[kwin-tuh-sen-shuhl]
adjective
1. of the pure and essential essence of something
2. of or pertaining to the most perfect embodiment of something

I can't say I'm pure or perfect, but I woke up that day gosh-darn fascinated by the idea of knowledge accumulated and how we can use what we've learned to be start a shared conversation. I grabbed a pen and scribed the first 47 things that came to mind. Then I realized, discovery is never done, it is what we do.

Props & Praise

To Max, who first made me aware of the quintessential 47.

To Jodi SuperGenius, who held my hand, brought her gift,and laughed every step of the way on this book.

To Blessed Mari of the Margaritas, my eleventh hour angel, for whom the only acceptable answer was "awesome!"

To Tiny Beast, who gave me pause, and wisdom beyond words.

To my Ninjas, you know who you are.

photo: Ryan Haro

Deena Ebbert is Propellergirl

International Speaker / Inspirational Author
Traveling the globe, provoking momentum,
and sharing conversations about living,
learning, and loving what we do.
propellergirl.com

Made in the USA
Middletown, DE
01 May 2021

38078681R00066